Discovering a New Way

possibilities for world peace in the patterns of our past

Discovering a

New Way

possibilities for world peace
in the patterns of our past

Ruth L. Miller

Discovering a New Way: possibilities for world
peace in the patterns of our past
© 2003, 2009, 2020 by Ruth L. Miller

Current edition published by Portal Center Press
Oregon, USA
www.portalcenterpress.com

ISBN: 978-1-936902-34-7

Ebook isbn: 978-1-936902-35-4

A few things we need to un-learn…

MYTH: Human beings have always lived by the rule of force and violence.

MYTH: A man's victories have always been the most important things in his life.

MYTH: Women have always (except in modern cities) been uninformed and powerless.

MYTH: War is inevitable.

MYTH: Oil's highest and best use is as fuel.

MYTH: History proves all of the above.

Contents

The American Way 1

The Anatolian Way 7

    Invasion & Empire: The Caucasian Way 17

    Modern Waves in the Pattern 26

From Herders to Empire-builders - A Possible
Explanation 33

    Observing Transition Points 36

    Growing Up Without Guidance 37

    Taking Wives 40

    A New Kind of Culture 41

    Continuing Today 44

Shifts in Understanding 47

Considering a New Way 55

    Seeking an Answer 59

    From Command-Control to Community 61

    From Conflict to Cooperation 64

    A Longer View 65

Looking Forward to a Possibility 67

    Oil as a Starting Point 67

    Design through Participation 69

    Clarifying our Intentions 70

    Necessary Resources 72

    Acquiring the Missing Pieces 74

    Coming to an Agreement 75

    Making it Work 76

    Envisioning Completion 80

Afterword 83

    The View from 2020 83

About the Author 87

American culture is becoming a global culture—with both wonderful and awful results. It's time we take a look at what American culture is based on, what it has become, and why. Once we understand that, we have a chance at ending war in the world and establishing prosperous, enjoyable, and creatively challenging lives for all humanity.

Foreword

This little book is a summary of research and design done between 2003 and 2012, expanded and updated with new information for 2020. In a series of short chapter-essays, it explores a different view of history and prehistory, and some future possibilities. It's based on evidence and arguments that aren't easily found in the mainstream literature, to explain current cultural norms that have not been explained – or often even recognized – in that literature.

The hope is that, as we understand more clearly why what we've been taught is inaccurate and inadequate for the current time, we can let it go and move on to a way of thinking and living that will ensure that humanity thrives on this planet – and beyond.

Some of this material was explored in greater detail in my book *Mary's Power*, where I attempted to explain the nature of feminine spiritual power and what has happened to it during the past 5000+ years of invasion and empire. You'll find references to that work in the text.

The final chapter in this book is based on a set of guidelines developed by extending what has worked in many communities and organizations to the international level. It duplicates, in part, the processes used by nations for their space missions and some military efforts. It's offered as a potential map for accomplishing the one, fundamental change that, in today's world, could actually unite humanity in a step toward living in harmony with our home, Earth.

In this work my goal is to provide a new framework, a new way of thinking about what is possible, so that we can all thrive – because, really, there is no reason for us not to!

~ Ruth L. Miller, April 2020

The American Way

Americans are very strange people, according to the rest of the world. We work longer hours with fewer benefits than almost any other people, we have more things than we can hold onto and seem to value them more than our personal comfort or relationships with the people around us, and not only do we not value the past, we're constantly destroying it as we work for an imaginary world called "the future."

In most cultures and the nations they form, these priorities are reversed. Time with family and in sacred community is very important (even in the "Dark Ages" each year had 160 "holy days," when shops were closed and fields were empty), and in most of industrial Europe, today, a 30-hour work week with 6-8 weeks of "holiday" is normal. In most places on this planet, who one is related to defines one's well-being and status in a community, almost regardless of the things one has. And, in virtually 90% of human cultures, the "living" past (alive in memory and story) defines present circumstances and the future exists only as a mirror of what one does today ("will our children's children speak well of us?").

Americans' focus on working hard to "make the future better" is not only strange, but threatening to most of Earth's peoples. They don't understand it. Moreover, it seems to undermine all that is important to their sense of wellbeing: the sacred traditions that have kept them well for centuries. It threatens most people, that is, except for the young men who don't feel adequately challenged within their communities. Young men, everywhere, love America and all that Americans make and do and stand for in the world. And, as (American) feminism spreads, more young women do, too.

Think about it. America was created by well-educated men in their 20s and early 30s (the "fathers of our country" were barely old enough to be fathers, themselves!) who were not satisfied with the *status quo*. The explorers who mapped our shores were typically the same age. Virtually all of the inventions we're so proud of were made by men in the same age range. Most of our heroes and celebrities are young men (or women who work to make their bodies look as youthful as possible)—in fact, in America, a man of 40 is considered "over the hill" and a woman over 30 is often considered "too old" for positions in the media or athletics – and in some businesses.[1]

America's attraction to youth and "what's new" shows up in every aspect of our culture. An item over 25 years old may be sold as an "antique." School and government buildings and factories are torn down and replaced after 40-50 years. Houses and business buildings built more than 20 years ago are likely to "need remodeling" and, if more than 40 years old, are often torn down to start over. Products must change their "look" every few years to "keep up with the times"—and with the market. And songs that were popular 5-10 years ago are "oldy-mouldies," while new sounds and new rhythms are "today's hits."

It's exciting to live in a world where everything is constantly changing, constantly being renewed! And it's this very excitement that attracts young men and women from all over the world to the American dream.

These young people, wanting to "get out on their own," feel stifled by the often ancient traditions that set the pace of life in their old communities. They don't see beauty in centuries-old buildings—they just see age. They don't

---

[1] Recently, with various anti-aging technologies, this is changing. For example Oprah Winfrey, America's leading daytime-media lady, has declared 50 to be "the new 30."

want to participate in the same old rituals, wearing the same clothes and doing the same things as their parents and grandparents.

This really shouldn't be surprising. At twenty-something, a man or woman is strong and energetic, has learned most of what can be taught by the community, and disagrees with a lot of it. This is the age of invention, the age of revolution—the age when most people come to America.

They come to "build a better life for themselves" and their families. They come with few resources beyond their willingness to try new things. They build new businesses and new homes. They buy new cars and the latest toys. They revel in the novelties they find here, and they send many "back home," enticing even more to come to this "land of golden opportunities."

Meanwhile, the folks back home worry. What's happening to their young people? Why don't they value the important things in life? Why do they go away and come back so different? What will become of the old, familiar way of life? And America begins to be seen as a threat—and a drain on their community.

In some ways they're right. Many of the young people—typically, "second sons" who see no real opportunity for expansion in "the old country"—never return. They marry Americans and choose the American lifestyle. They have children and do everything they can to raise those children as Americans, focused on a wonderful future life rather than the present or past, learning as little history as possible, and barely acknowledging that they have family in other countries: relatives who speak a different language and have a rich cultural tradition that goes back centuries.

So their children, grandchildren, and great-grandchildren have no idea what their family's traditions have been and no understanding of the language of their ancestors, and they as-sume—even expect—that everyone in the world will look and talk and act just like they do in America.

So, for nearly 400 years, there's been a new wave of immigrants every few years: the Brit-ish, the Irish, the Germans, the Africans (by force), the Scandinavians, the Italians, the Chinese (too many by force), the Russian and European Jews, the Puerto Ricans, the Viet-namese, the Mexicans, and lately the Arabs and East Indians. These, and almost every oth-er nation in between, have sent their young people to be part of what's happening in this amazing country—and all have lost much in our "melting pot."

At first, the newcomers struggle against barriers of custom, prejudice, and language.

Then, often within a generation, their offspring have contributed something wonderful and new to their new country, and the ongoing revolution that is the American Way.

The Anatolian Way

One of the delightful ironies of American culture is that our obsession with the latest and greatest has led us to invent some wonderful tools for understanding the ancient past. Twenty-first century archaeology is a high-tech operation that has very little in common with 19th century "digs" (except that dirt and rocks and layers of artifacts continue to be moved and sifted and documented, usually under a hot sun, somewhere "in the middle of nowhere.") With the new technologies, as might be expected, some old assumptions about the development of our culture are being turned upside down.

For an archaeologist two thousand years from now, tracing America's cultural roots would be an absolute nightmare. A true "melting pot," America is a constantly changing blend of ideas and artifacts from all over the world. In spite of our educational institutions' efforts to ground all of us in "Western Civilization," we speak and work and believe and act on the basis of increasingly cross-cultural norms. Our language, though based on English, is barely recognizable to the average "Brit"—mostly because of our pronunciation, but also because of all the technical terms and "slang" (including idioms from other cultures) built into it. Our music is a wonderful blend of European, African, Latin American and Asian musical traditions. Our forms of the world's religions are based on, but often quite different from, the originals in other countries—offering a unique blend of rituals and even dogmas, emerging from interaction with other traditions. The things we use in our homes may have originated any place in the world: like rice cookers, porcelain, and barbecues from East Asia; pajamas, paisley cloth, and madras shirts from India; teak furniture from Scandinavia or Southeast Asia; ceiling fans from Africa. The foods we eat come from every continent, even "traditionally American" things like peanuts (Africa), hot dogs and hamburgers (Germany), sweet potatoes (Indonesia), and apple pie (England and Germany). And new things from new places are being introduced every year.

By contrast, most archaeologists find that the cultures of most other places around the world have remained pretty much the same for centuries. With a few exceptions (usually coastal cities), most villages and towns have grown slowly, with little innovation, over long periods of time. They find a pattern that is sustainable and they keep it. And the further back we go in time, the more slowly things changed.

One of the earliest town-sites to be excavated is in Asia Minor, the region once known as Anatolia.[2] It's so old that some have called it the missing link between the ancient hunting culture and the village farming culture of the "Fertile Crescent."[3] With an average population of about 1000 people, the town, known as Catal-Huyuk, was occupied for over 5000 years, evolving from a village of scattered huts with shared gardens (about 9000bce) to a well-planned town with covered sewers, plastered-brick houses with doors and courtyards, and open plazas, by 6000bce. There are remains of many kinds of foods, with shared food-storage facilities. There are copper implements and jewelry, alongside beautifully worked stone and pottery, and some of the pottery and stonework have a form of "sacred script" on them. Most strikingly, for hundreds of years at a time, according to an analysis of burial remains, no one died a violent death.

---

[2] There is no formal "Anatolian" culture, simply a set of sites in that region of Asia Minor, but the time-period and commonality with other cultures make it a useful "tag" for the kind of culture being described here.

[3] Among others, James Mellart of the British Institute of Archaeology at Ankara, the Neolithic of the Near East (1975), quoted in Riane Eisler's The Chalice and the Blade, pp 7-10.

Like most other sites of what's called the "neolithic" era ("new stone," age of gardeners, in contrast to the paleolithic, "old stone" age of hunting-gathering tribes), the religious artifacts at Catal-Huyuk focus on a triune feminine presence, maiden-mother-crone, as the source and sustainer of all, sometimes with a son and a lover alongside her. Wall paintings, pottery, and jewelry show various interactions of these icons: Virgin-Maiden alone or with a serpent, bull, or moon, Mother bearing all life, Maiden and lover, Mother with infant Son, lover as hunter, Son injured and dying, Crone alone or with the waning moon or a bull or restoring her Son's life, etc.

These icons illustrate the same stories that are written and told, even today, about the goddess and her modern forms. Christians honor the Virgin Mary, Mother of God, who holds her infant Son as the *Madonna* (Great Mother) and her dying Son in the statues called *pieta* (meaning piety, faithfulness) and ascends into heaven to be with him after his resurrection. Muslims honor Fatima, the Blessed Prophet Mohammed's (not historically documented) daughter, whose name means "Mother of her Father" and is also the name of the Moon-goddess in the Medina area of Arabia. The Islamic fast of *Ramadhan* continues the age-old tradition of fasting while the goddess

weeps for her dead lover/son in winter, and the
Jewish *Rosh Hashanna* (meaning "head of the
year") is the age-old fast of atonement, making
it possible for the risen Son of the Goddess
(new plants) to return with the rains of the new
year (celebrated under various names around
the fall equinox throughout the Middle East).
Christians and pagans throughout Europe observe Easter (a translation of *Oestre*—the root
for estrogen and related female terms) as the
resurrection of life on the first Sunday after the
first full moon after the vernal equinox. Even
the Hebrew *Shekinah* ("the Presence," literally,
"to dwell, abide") is described in Goddess
terms: "waxing and waning moon... well wa-
ters... lily of the valley, Mother Wisdom... gate-
way and door... mother eagle, serpent... the
Sabbath Queen and Bride, the Tree of Life, the
menorah, and the earth itself."[4]

The ubiquity of these images and stories
isn't surprising. Comparing the town-pattern,
art forms, and tools of Catal-Huyuk with other
sites in Europe and the Middle East, it looks as
if the culture of Anatolia spread, over several
thousand years, across Macedonia and north-
ward into Europe, southward along the Mediterranean coast, onto the islands of Crete and

---

[4] Lynn Gottlieb, *She Who Dwells Within* (1995),
pp.20-22.

Cyprus, and eastward through Mesopotamia and into India. Jericho and other ancient Palestinian sites repeat this pattern. Early Egyptian villages repeat this pattern. Sites along the Danube River do, as well. Between 8000bce[5] and 5000bce, everywhere a river created a fertile flood plain, the Anatolian pattern emerged. And with this pattern we see artifacts of that same triune (maiden-mother-crone) goddess religion, evident in every home and public area.[6]

In or near these towns are usually found two significant pieces of architecture. One is the stone circle, oriented to the sun, moon, and evening star, and often built on a hill under which a "blind spring" (underground water source, feeding other springs in the area) is located. The stones making up these circles vary in size, from mere boulders to the huge stones we find in places like Stonehenge outside of Salisbury, England. Similar megalithic stone

---

[5] "bce" means "before the common era." Previously it would have been written as B.C., meaning "before Christ." The Roman Empire was established about the same time so historians made the switch when the universities were no longer run by the churches but by the State.

[6] This understanding of such findings was pioneered by University of California archeologist Marija Gimbutas and is documented in *The Goddesses and Gods of Old Europe*. Riane Eisler, Monica Sjoo, and other feminist writers have drawn extensively on her work.

circles can be found throughout Europe, the Mideast, and the Americas, and have been dated in Brittany as early as 4000bce.

The other common structure is the temple mound, with three rings of courtyards before an inner chamber that has one small door and no windows, the interior walls of which were usually painted with red ochre or ox-blood. These, too, are found from Egypt and Mesopotamia to Yorkshire, dating as early as 5000bce.

Based on illustrations and more recent structures of the same style, it seems that the first, largest courtyard was a place where anyone might gather, at any time, to bring gifts, hear the stories, dance the dances, and enjoy the blessings of the goddess and her son and consort. The second, slightly smaller courtyard, was only for those who had been initiated (literally meaning "begun, introduced") into the sacred community, and teachers and healers would meet with students, disciples, aspirants there, providing esoteric (meaning "inner circle") knowledge. The smallest, interior courtyard was restricted to those who had demonstrated a willingness and ability to learn and serve: priests, priestesses, and their novice-assistants. Here rituals were prepared and occult (meaning "hidden") teachings were shared. Within this courtyard, the inner sanctum, the "Holy of Holies," was kept sacred (which means "set apart"). Only someone who was in direct communion with the divine could enter this blood-colored chamber and expect to come out alive. And only on certain days of the year was it necessary to enter.

Those sacred days, according to the stories and illustrations, were determined by the position of the sun and moon and the season of the year—often figured from their alignment in the stone circle. If those who tracked the night skies saw that it was time to give thanks for harvest, or to cause the rains to start, then it would be necessary for the priest/priestess to commune with the goddess. On rare occasions, it might be necessary to enter the sacred space to find guidance for the community—as did the priestess, or oracle, at Delphi. Part of the initiation process of the priest/priestess was, according to Egyptian records and later stories in Mesopotamia, to be sealed into this "inner sanctum" for three days and nights, to rise again as a new being, part human and part divine, able to "sit at the right hand" (an idiom that means "manage the work") of the Goddess.

That work varied from community to community, depending on the number of people, the amount of land needed to sustain them, and the storage requirements for food. In smaller communities, of a few hundred or less, the priestess/priest would act as mediator and arbitrator for whatever conflicts might arise, as well as chief healer—living out the role of the goddess (or her consort) for everyone. In larger communities (sometimes as many as several thousand), these roles would be distributed among many well-trained people.

One of the interesting things about these towns is that there doesn't seem to be a hierarchy; there's no great difference in wealth among the residents. While some homes have priestly objects and others have artisan's tools, for hundreds and thousands of years, houses, jewelry and other art forms, food storage and preparation areas are all similar in size, number, and capacity. The Anatolian pattern of community appears to have been very egalitarian.

It was also very inventive. Not only were baked bricks, plastering, tiles, chimneys, covered sewers, and other ceramics well advanced by the 8th millennium bce, metallurgy began in these communities, so that by the time Crete was settled around 4500bce (their capital, Knossos, was built about 2500bce), ceramic, bronze, and copper implements were common.

While lack of machinery required various forms of manual labor, making life physically challenging for everyone, it was a peaceful time, a time of comfort, beauty, and stability that lasted over 4000 years in Anatolia, and still continues today in some isolated regions. But as all things do in this world, that age came to an end, as the Bronze "Age of Marauders" unfolded.

Invasion & Empire: The Caucasian Way

The first major change away from the Anatolian village way of life occurred about 6,000 years ago, around 4000bce, when the first significant wave of raiders came out of the Caucasus mountains.

These young, light-haired men, calling themselves "Sons of Light," preferred tent-camps over towns and weapons over jewelry, and they sought range-lands for their herds, not recognizing fenced gardens as useful. They rode horses and, in later years, used chariots and donkey carts.

They had little use for "women's ways" and lived by stories about the heroic accomplishments of great men, telling of the animals and people they'd killed, the monsters they'd bested, and the number of children born to them. (The earliest of these stories were compiled in the *Rig Veda*, about 2000 years later.)

They wanted land for their ever-growing herds and women to bear them children, and counted the number of cattle and people they controlled as a measure of their greatness.[7]

Based on similar encounters in recent history it's likely that, in the egalitarian and inclusive cultures of the garden-based river towns, the first groups of Caucasian herders were probably welcomed, and a place made for them adjacent (or in) the settlements. But the ways of these new arrivals were so different (honoring warriors and cattle, discounting gardens and women, as they did) and their numbers grew so fast, that what at first may have been a neighborly adjustment soon took the form of an invasion.

These people of the Caucasus mountains are sometimes called Aryans and usually called "Indo-European" because their language became the basis for nearly all the languages from Scotland to India. Today, Caucasians are everywhere, and their light hair and skin is still considered a mark of privilege and class, around the world. Their expansion out of the

---

[7] Lest the following section be viewed as a polemic against a specific race, the author's background is pure American mongrel: light skin and reddish-brown hair proves Caucasian ancestry (through the British Isles, France, and Germany), high cheekbones and epicanthal folds demonstrate a significant portion of Native American "blood," a Semitic nose comes from a Jewish grandparent, and curly hair comes from a Virginian ancestor who was born in the slave quarters.

rugged mountains of their origin has transformed the lives of all of humanity—and not always for the better.

That first wave of Caucasian invasions wiped out many towns and villages in the Near East, and Anatolian refugees moved westward into Europe and southward toward the Greek isles, Mesopotamia, and Egypt. Women were absorbed into Caucasian families and the time-honored goddess stories they brought with them were blended with the Caucasion hero stories.

Some of the settled peoples were able to save their towns, but only by letting the Caucasian warrior-herders take over as "headmen" rulers. In such cases, it seems that an amicable arrangement was worked out in which the Goddess remained, but the Caucasian chief became her consort—typically, by "marrying" (usually more like taking ownership of) the priestess who represented the Goddess.

In this way a new kind of leadership was founded. Instead of a periodic mystical union with the divine as the source of guidance for decision-making, the very human understandings and knowledge of Caucasian headmen became the daily rule—balanced insofar as possible by the priestess' wisdom. Then, as the chief's offspring replaced the priestesses, the rituals were changed, and with them the stories: Caucasian heroes were now called the Mother Goddess' father, son, or husband—or all three.

From this a new, hierarchical social structure developed, with the blond Caucasians (the "Sons of light") at the top, controlling the resources and making decisions for the masses (who, according to later records, called themselves "children of earth"). These populations, over generations, accepted their new rulers with the modifications of the old religion and the new names and values that came with them. They also accepted their new roles, as specialists in the "machine" of the empire, producing just one thing to meet the needs of the whole population, according to the demands of the rulers—instead of using a variety of skills to produce the variety of goods used by individual households as they had before.

At the same time, though, the new rulers were at least partially assimilated into the local culture, with their children and grandchildren adopting many of the town's traditions as their own. So each empire became a new hybrid culture, with Caucasian elements and remnants of the Anatolian pattern.[8]

---

[8] This pattern is still visible in India, where remnants remain of the Muslim invasions and assimilation into Hindu culture, as well as the British invasions.

As the populations in the Caucasus continued to grow (lots of children was a good thing in their culture, unlike the Anatolians), the need for range-land increased, and the second measurable wave of invasions occurred around 3300bce. This time, the invaders had the bronze implements and other aids they'd acquired from the Anatolians in earlier invasions.

Then, around 3000bce, 600-800 years after the process first began to be visible in the archeological record, came the third big wave, which scholars call the *Jamna.*

They made their way across the Fertile Crescent and up into the Danube valley, and also moved north and eastward, taking over the steppes all the way to Mongolia, and into China. Records indicate that the *Jamna* wave of Aryans into Europe and the Near East was paralleled by a new *Jomon* culture in Japan. About the same time, Huang-ti, China's first emperor (2697bce), was called "the Yellow Emperor" by his dark-skinned people—beginning a tradition there that to have light-colored skin is to be more beautiful and "higher class."

After that, every few decades, a new wave of invasions expanded the Caucasian territory: into the garden-centered towns along the Tigris and Euphrates in Mesopotamia, and along the Nile in Egypt. Each wave of Caucasian invasions resulted in changes to the old way of life,

wherever they went. How much change de-
pended on whether they came directly out of
the Caucasus or simply were expanding their
holdings into their neighbors' lands.
The same pattern occurred everywhere. If
the people were willing to let the Caucasians
take over, their town survived. If not, it was
flattened and turned into range-land, with the
young women carried off and the rest killed or
driven into hiding. So, with each wave a new,
hybrid culture with a new name would emerge.

The people of lower Mesopotamia, who
called themselves "the black-haired people," integrated the Caucasian stories into their pre-
existing Goddess stories and were able to inte-
grate the light-skinned blond Caucasian leaders fairly painlessly (i.e., few towns and temples
were destroyed) in the pattern that had worked
elsewhere: "marrying" the wise elder priestess
with the big light-skinned headman.

This meant that, by the middle of the 4th
millennium bce, in what became Sumeria, the
written work ("sacred script") of the temples
was not lost in the process (as it had been in
too many other places) and evolved into the
famous wedge-shaped "cuneiform" writing on
clay tablets that is considered the basis for all
writing, today. The clearly Caucasian epic "Gil-
gamesh," describing the heroic exploits of a
larger-than-normal man who took what he

wanted, totally ignored the area's social norms, and was determined to become immortal, was first written in that script about 3000bce.

After that, the records indicate that every few decades, a new wave of invasions expanded the Caucasian territory, into the garden-centered towns along the Tigris and Euphrates in Mesopotamia and along the Nile in Egypt, transforming every community along the way.

According to those records, a brief summary of the process in Egypt could be described as:

- Fair-skinned "Menes the Fighter" united the upper and lower districts of Egypt around 3000bce, ending the town system and the reign of the Moon-Goddess.
- A few years later invasions by Caucasian-Semitic Assyrians took over Palestine and then Mesopotamia, and the Caucasian-Anatolian Phoenicians took over the Syrian coast—both harassing the Egyptians for centuries thereafter.
- The Hyksos (Semitic "shepherd kings") invaded and ruled northern Egypt for 500 years, starting about 2000bce.
- A wealthy cattle-herding Semite from Mesopotamia named Abram brought his sister-wife Serai for a visit and was honored as royalty; his great-grandson Joseph was so highly regarded that he was

second only to the pharaoh, as Vizier, about 1800bce.

- The Semitic Hyksos pharaoh-kings were overcome by Ahmose, a descendent of southern Egyptian pharaohs, around 1550bce, deposing the Semitic rulers and their friends and families, who were used as a labor force for some years, to be led out by the adopted Semitic prince, Moses.[9]

- For the next thousand years Egypt's rulers fought with and took on wives from neighboring kingdoms in a constant effort to maintain control over the Nile valley.

- Around 330bce the Caucasian Alexander's Macedonian army took over the region and Egypt was ruled by Greeks well into the Roman empire.

Following the same timeline in the East, Caucasian invaders (known there as "Aryans") reached the Indus valley by 2150bce, and destroyed the goddess-oriented gardening towns along that river, to replace them with tent encampments and pastures for cattle. The *Rig Veda* includes an account of that invasion,

---

[9] Tradition has it that the Exodus occurred in the reign of Rameses the Great, but the archeological and geological records suggest it may have been much earlier – perhaps even in the reign of Ahmose I.

written in an early form of Sanskrit, and was soon established as the basis for the religious doctrine of the Indian sub-continent. There, the invaders established a caste system with themselves at the top, as priests and warriors, and everyone else below them, the dark-skinned natives being considered "untouchable" by the pure "Sons of Light." And, although the warriors were replaced by the priests a thousand year later, still, in India today, as throughout Asia, light skin is preferable over dark skin—considered more beautiful and "higher class."

Along the Danube, over the same years, the Anatolian culture was taken over by Caucasian-Kurgans, overlaying their warrior model on the towns' goddess-garden model, and leading to the formation of the Baden culture. As a result, by 2500bce, a new, integrated culture, identified by its characteristic "corded pottery" was established in the Rhine valley with very similar spin-off groups as far north as Scandinavia and the Upper Volga.[10]

So, thanks to new archeological tools, our picture of the process by which "civilization" (which means "living in cities") came to be is very different from the one most Americans have been taught in school. Between the ar-

[10] From Marija Gimbutas, *The Indo-Europeans in the Third and Fourth Millenia* (1982).

cheological evidence and the historical record, it's clear that there was a high quality of life in the towns and villages along the various rivers of Europe, Asia, and North Africa for thousands of years before the warrior-Caucasians arrived with their "new inventions" of invasion, divine right to rule, and empire, destroyed much of what was in place, and established the empire-kingdoms of Mesopotamia, India, and Egypt.

More, it seems that much of what has been passed down as the "inventions" of those early kingdoms are the remains of what had been in place prior to the invasions. This picture is re-inforced by the continuation of goddess-oriented rituals at the turn of the seasons (especially that of the ancient Sumerian goddess' lover, Tammuz, prior to the rains) through the Roman era, and still practiced by Semitic peoples of all faiths, even today.

Modern Waves in the Pattern

Following the historical record, this pattern of waves of invasion and new empire-building every couple hundred years continues well into the modern period. [11]

---

[11] The pattern is trace-able in any timeline of world history and is detailed in the appendix to my book, *Mary's Power*. Why about 200 years apart? Because it takes that long for a culture to "forget" its roots and the pain of invasion? It takes that long to fill up a region to

Historians trace our current version of this culture of invasion and empire back to 348bce, when Philip of Macedon, proud of his Caucasian ancestry and determined to bring his particular brand of civilization to the rest of the world, began to build his empire. His blond son, Alexander, went on to defeat the Persian emperor, Darius, in battle, which gave him title to the Persian empire, including lands all the way to the Indus and down the length of the Nile. And, although his empire fell apart at Alexander's death just a few years later, his Greek generals divided it up and continued their control, so the Macedonian and Greek influence on those regions is still felt today.

Meanwhile, Rome, a set of towns built on the hills around the river Tiber and dedicated to the Goddess (symbolized by a mother wolf who suckled the heroes Romulus and Remus), had been taken over by Caucasians expanding their territory across the peninsula. These men established a caste system and replaced the divinely anointed leader with a pair of consuls who were elected by the invaders: men who owned property.

These new, warrior Romans were fighting battles on several fronts throughout the third century bce, protecting themselves from Gauls

---

the point where more space (or challenge) is needed,

(Caucasian-Badens to the north), Carthaginians (Phoenician-Caucasians to the south and east), and the long-established EtruscanCaucasians next door.

Once the Roman generals had taken over most of Italy, they moved into Gaul and Spain, destroyed Corinth and Carthage, and took over Greece in 147bce. That gave them control of the empire Alexander had won, from Egypt to the Indus. The empire-building process was underway—right on the 200-year schedule.

Then, as happens to all empires, the people who'd been conquered changed the conquerors, so something new emerged. Because of extensive written records, we can see the progression for Rome. Having been a goddess-focused town (*Roma* is a feminine word), the Romans' ideal model for decision-making was at least nominally egalitarian—and all citizens were entitled to a vote. As an empire, however, there needed to be a "commander-in-chief" who had sufficient authority to manage thousands of troops from dozens of cultures. Julius, the general who called himself Caesar, decided to revert to the old formula for kingship and married the great goddess Juno's high priestess, which, at that time, entitled him to call himself a divine Son of the Goddess. His successor, Octavius

---

elsewhere? Tied to some planetary cycle?

(who also married the high priestess and called himself Augustus), was therefore the "Son of God" as were all the emperors to follow.

In this way, simple, egalitarian, almost-democratic Rome became the spiritual, financial, and military capital of a huge empire—which was far more than its urbane citizens could handle.

But their leaders and most of their famous legions were Caucasian warriors, with a mythos of heroic deeds and conquests, a commitment to expanding their territory to ensure lands for their sons, and the belief that safety lay in controlling the world around them. So the empire continued to grow and the city became overwhelmed with peoples and ideas from all over the world.

Along about 50ce, a number of things began to shift. In the northern provinces, tribes of Caucasian-Goths were uniting and forming a kingdom of their own. In the province of Syria (which included Judea and Israel) a strange new religion was growing which insisted that some Palestinian Jew was the "Son of God," rather than honoring the emperor as such. In response to these threats, plus overcrowding, the city was to see 10 emperors over the next 50 years, many of whom were poisoned.

Then the upstart Trajan, a Caucasian "plebe" (not one of the original ruling families) born in Spain, moved up through the military ranks and managed to expand the empire to its greatest extent, from England into Arabia, between 98 and 116ce. His reign was the last time those regions were peaceful for almost 2000 years.

So the waves of conquest continued—all the way through the emergence of Islam and the Medieval and Renaissance periods in Europe, and around the world. And each new conqueror, like generations of invaders before them, offered towns the option of being captured and assimilated into the invader's way of living, or destroyed.

A new wave began in the 1500s, with the European-Caucasian invasion of Africa and the Americas and the same options were imposed. The light-skinned European-Americans enslaved thousands of dark-skinned Africans and destroyed virtually the total population of dark-skinned native peoples who had occupied the Americas, continuing the age-old Caucasian pattern – and teaching it to people of other races in the parts of the world they had invaded.

Then the American Revolution happened, along with a reduction in European slavery, and the period from 1775 through 1845 saw new kinds of governments form in Europe, based on constitutions and law, rather than divine rights of kings. The European rulers continued to invade other continents and fight over lands and resources, but only the small, dark, up-start Napoleon Bonaparte tried to take over other countries in Europe. And he was thoroughly squashed.

It was the mid-1900s before an elected leader who was not "of the blood"—not part of the intermarried royal families of Europe— broke the "gentlemen's agreement" and actually set out to conquer his neighboring countries. Interestingly, this small, black-haired Semite did so in the name of reclaiming Europe for the tall, blond "Sons of Light:" the Caucasians whom he called Aryans.

From Herders
to Empire-builders -
A Possible Explanation

The process of individual human development has been studied from many perspectives over the ages. Probably the best "experts" on the subject are grandparents and great-grandparents who have observed themselves and their friends, their children and their neighbors' children, and their grandchildren and the young people around them over several decades. Recently, we also have the results of several well-documented "longitudinal" studies of individuals and families over 40 to 70 years. Of course, both forms of information are limited by the questions being asked and the perspectives of those answering, but across the board, there are some interesting insights to be gained.

First, it's clear that humans go through several well-defined developmental stages, as described in many developmental textbooks. Briefly, regardless of where they're raised, for the first six months, human beings simply take in the world around them. The next year is spent attempting to learn more by interacting with that world. By age two, children everywhere have decided who they are and how the world works and begin to assert themselves in the household. By age 5, they have mastered most of the language and basic social skills necessary for social survival. Around age 7, they're working out rational explanations for what, heretofore, they've simply accepted as how life is; they start asking new kinds of questions and exploring new kinds of experience. As puberty kicks in, they start to explore relationships in new ways and identify strongly with their peer group. By adolescence, they're physically mature and feel ready to strike out on their own—but are still lacking in neurological connections and may not yet have the strength or skills to do so, so they enter a "push me-pull you" relationship with their parents and community. In their twenties, virtually everybody "has all the answers"—whether they do or not. (There's a reason the President of the U.S. has to be over 35!). And this is usually when they launch a career or move to a new country.

Second, the way we move through those stages is defined, in part, by the family and community and larger culture in which we live. In some cultures, for example, adolescence lasts only a few months, and by 13 or 14 one is considered an adult, able to marry, create a home, and raise children. By contrast, in the U.S. and industrialized Europe, adolescence is significantly prolonged—to as late as 21, 22, or even 26 years of age, depending on the length of time spent in school and job-training.

Another very interesting point about human development that's beginning to be understood is that if one has not adequately completed a stage—if trauma, addiction, or some other event caused one to skip part of a stage—one will, at some point in life, "revert" and complete that stage. (Related to that understanding is the realization that, soon after being widowed or divorced, people who've been married for a long time will typically revert to the emotional stage they were in at the time they were married.)

These insights suggest that adults who seem to be acting like children or teenagers may well be doing so—they may be reverting to an incomplete stage—and need to be allowed to, or they'll be stuck in that stage for the rest of their lives. The research also suggests that children and teens who are not allowed to "act their age" at the appropriate stage will do so later.

Observing Transition Points

The members of long-term, sustainable cultures understand these things. They use a set of procedures and traditions to ensure that everyone moves through the appropriate stages at the appropriate ages, with activities and support for doing so smoothly, and with little hassle for all concerned.

Early anthropologists discovered some of these processes and called them "rites of passage." They saw the people of the villages they were studying do special things at specific times in a person's life and reported these practices in their theses and journal articles, sometimes wondering if European-Americans would not benefit from something like them. Among the "rites" that have been reported are: the vision quest, in which an adolescent is sent out into the wilderness to struggle and fast and discover the vision that will guide his (rarely her) life. Others include: circumcision; tattooing and piercing to fit the pattern of the family, clan, or tribe; special dances, and ritual hunts or raids. Others, more familiar to European-Americans, include weddings, naming ceremonies, and funerals.

Each of these processes helps people move through the stages from childhood into adulthood and beyond, offering activities that fit their physical and emotional state, while preparing them to identify themselves as responsible adult members of the community. They help to maintain the balance—in the individual and for the community as a whole. Some of them remind the parents that their children are no longer theirs to guide or direct. Still others provide an outlet for hormones that might otherwise be dangerous within the community.[12] All of them teach people to face their fears and discover that what they feared is not as bad as their imaginations led them to believe.

Sometimes, though, the necessary activities don't happen. Perhaps there's been a crisis and the adults don't have the time to create the appropriate experience for a particular age group. Perhaps there's been an illness or a disaster and there are no adults around who remember how to help the children become responsible and well-balanced members of the community.

Growing Up Without Guidance

It's easy to imagine how, in a herding culture that sends its young boys up a mountain with the goats or sheep or cattle, there might be a storm or a flood or a landslide that separates a group of boys from their parents and siblings. One can imagine how these seven-, eight-, nine- and ten-year old boys would feel

---

[12] Some specific examples of these are described in detail in my book *Mary's Power*.

when they headed back home—and found there was no home there, anymore. Their emotions would run the gamut from terror to determination to find a way to loneliness to homesickness to renewed terror and, ultimately, grief—and with it all, anger and denial.

Then hunger would set in. The older boys would know a little more about how to survive and would either help the younger ones or taunt and tease them with their superior skills. Depending on the season, there would probably be precious little to eat without sacrificing one of the animals they were charged with protecting. A moral dilemma, for sure—and no adults to advise them!

Fear would be the dominant emotion for these boys: fear of predators, fear of the weather, fear of going hungry, and fear of other boys who might prevent them from getting what they need—or even hurt them. If one of them were sick or injured, the others may or may not help him. If one of them found a good supply of food, he may or may not share it with the others. Clearly, the strongest and most knowledgeable boy would be looked up to by the others. They would listen to his stories of how to do things and how successful he was at doing them, and the younger, weaker ones would aim to be protected by him.[13] They would learn, in the process, that the way to deal with being afraid is to dominate and control that which they feared.

Periodically, the boys would try to reconnect with their families. In some cases, they might find them and be welcomed home to warmth and loving arms—the nightmare over. In many, however, they would not. And, after a few months or years, they would stop trying.

Over those years they would be inventing a new culture—a combination of values and tools and ways of doing things that kept them going. That culture would be based on keeping the herd healthy and following the leadership of the strongest, most knowledgeable young man. It would be based on a deep bonding among the boys, a near-worship of the strongest among them (based in part, on fear that he'd beat them if they didn't), and a simple diet of the meat (and possibly milk) of the animals they herded, supplemented by occasional fruits, roots, or nuts. It would involve killing predators and controlling the unruly animals or boys with whatever means they had. And it would, after time, assume that whatever they found

---

[13] William Golding's *Lord of the Flies* is another thought experiment based on this idea.

was theirs for the taking simply because they needed or wanted it.

Taking Wives

After 5 years or so, the oldest boys would be well past puberty, and, though some homosexual activity was probable, hormones, combined with faded memories of watching other young men with the women "back home" and current observations of the herd animals, would drive the boys to find more people. So the band would set out on an arduous journey out of the mountains. They would follow a stream down to a river and follow the river until they found a trail to a village. Depending on their appearance and behavior, they might be welcomed by the people there, and maybe even given a place to live and keep their herd. Unskilled and ungroomed, they would be considered barbarians, wild men, almost animals.

Nonetheless, in some communities, there might be a family or group of families able and willing to take them in and adopt them. In others, such would not be the case. Often, based on still-existing stories, the boys would behave so outrageously as to cause the villagers to kick them out, or they would feel so uncomfortable with the villagers' "rules and restrictions" that they chose to leave. In either case, they probably would not leave without taking what they wanted—which probably included a young woman or two and some food, clothing, and tools.

After fleeing the village as they would flee from a predator in the mountains (or from an older boy trying to beat them), the young men and boys would have a choice. They could return to the mountains or they could continue to travel through the valley. Some would go back to the familiar high country, taking their women, their herd, and their new belongings with them, to make a home. Others, individually or as a group, would decide to stay in the valley and see what they could find, elsewhere. After a few such experiences, a new "rite of passage"—going into the villages to steal a woman—would have become firmly entrenched as this group's cultural norm. It would confirm one's strength as a "man" without ensuring that the necessary stages of development had been accomplished.

A New Kind of Culture

And so a culture based on the exploits of strong-bodied, emotionally immature male figures would emerge. Its members would have no need for permanent houses, feel free to take what they pleased, honor the strongest, and assume that anyone weaker was a lesser human being. That would mean that, as a man passed his prime, he was a target for the next strong youth to take his place. So there would be little respect for an older or injured man, and only the youthful, active men would be eligible for positions of leadership.

Also, because the only model for female that most of the boys had would be a vague memory of mother (tinged with anger at her disappearance) and observations of females in the herd, there would be no tradition of respect for women and the kinds of contributions women might make. And, since having lots of babies was good for the herd, it must be good for the band, as well. Keeping women "barefoot, pregnant and in the tent" would therefore be the norm—with the expectation that, of course, she would bear lots of small boys for him to rule and use to control others. Then, too, because women were a scarce commodity and easily stolen, a man would not want the other men to see his own, so he would insist that she cover herself completely when outside of the tent.

Inside the tent, a woman would be a sexual object and be expected to simultaneously atone for the sins of and fulfill the maternal role the boy had been deprived of when separated from his home. She would be expected to behave according to the rules that the band of boys had developed when on their own, or, as the boys probably had been, she'd be beaten for her infractions.

However, since the man's wants were few, what she did with her time when he was gone was her own. So the women got together. They talked about their old lives in the villages. They reminded each other about the goddess and the rituals and the dances. Sometimes they would dance for each other as they had in the village. And, on those few occasions when they menstruated (when they were not pregnant or nursing a baby), they would set up a special tent to be alone or with other menstruating women and allow the blood to flow into the earth, as they had been taught in their old home that it should, for the good of all. The women lived their lives and loved their children and did what was expected by their men—as much to avoid a beating as out of respect or affection— and passed on to their girls the lessons of their lives. And so the Caucasian-Semitic women's culture emerged, complementing, but almost completely separate from, the men's ideas and activities.[14]

When a new generation of boys were about the same age as their fathers had been when

---

[14] Recent documentaries of the lives of Middle Eastern and central Asian women made by western women confirm that such remains the case today.

separated from their families, they'd be sent off with the herds for a season or two, to "learn how to be men." And when there were too many people and animals for the local area to support, these strong, but emotionally stunted young men would be sent off to find new lands and new women.

Continuing Today

Sound familiar? Not too surprisingly, this description fits current Caucasian-Semitic culture norms very closely. This pattern of culture, which emerged out of the Caucasus mountains 6000 years ago, has dominated the Asian steppes and the region from the Mediterranean to the Indus, ever since. Regardless of religion or emperor or the Internet, it remains. Young boys are removed from their mother's care about the age of 7 and raised as their fathers and uncles were.[15] Wives are "stolen" from neighbors' families[16] and kept hidden from other men. Strangers are always both suspect and

---

[15] Interestingly, this is also the practice in British middle- and upper-class homes. Boys are sent off to boys' schools at age 7—and have been since about the 1500s. Prior to that they were sent off to work as pages at that age, following the traditional pattern of arranging for young boys to apprentice to a trade, which continued, even in the Americas, into the 1800s.

[16] In elaborate wedding rituals where the groom rides in and "takes" the bride away from her family.

a potential source of wealth. And the strongest man is in charge.

Behind and beneath this "man's world" are the fears of a young boy taken away from the comforts of mother and a nurturing community and made to rely on his wits and puny strength. And, since these men weren't able to move through the ages and stages of normal development, they now have to deal with those stages as adults.

So, throughout the regions dominated by Caucasian culture, we see the pattern of invasion and control, as the pre-adolescent boy strikes out in his man's body and declares "Look at me! Look how strong and wonderful I am!"—the very words recorded as spoken by many of the new kings and emperors in Mesopotamia for millennia. We see men living by controlling others, often using the law: harsh rules with harsher consequences. We see, as well, the destruction and discounting of older men as young men come in with greater strength.

Each new ruler has been supplanted by another. Each new empire has fallen to another. Each attempt to expand and control has failed in the long run, leaving ruined cities and scorched earth behind.

Even in this century, as the U.S. military toppled the regime of Sadaam Hussein in

Baghdad, the pattern continued. The men cheered in the streets for their new, younger, more powerful leader: "Bush! Bush!" they chanted—as they had chanted for Hussein less than a decade before. And, when it became clear that George W. Bush was not the leader they hoped for, a vacuum existed that many others have been fighting to fill, ever since.

Shifts in Understanding

The fundamental element of empire culture is the belief that we have to "own" a resource to have access to it. This means we have to "rule" over someone to rely on them. And it means we are constantly "protecting" what we believe is "ours" from others who want it – or from the one force we wish we could control but haven't yet: Nature. In the minds of empire-builders this is fact and history proves it.

Modern science, however, has been proving otherwise for the past century. As we've developed new tools for observing and testing the world around us over long periods of time, we've learned that this universe is not at all what we've been trained to believe it is.

The emergence of the systems sciences since the mid-20th century, including ecology, complexity theory, cybernetics, and more, has provided us with powerful tools for understanding how the world really works. Like any science, the field is rife with its own jargon, and like any science it has a mathematics of its own that must be learned to really work with the tools that have been discovered. There are, however, a few fundamental principles that require neither jargon nor mathematics to understand. These are:

- A system is a set of elements that work together in fulfillment of some purpose;
- Everything in any system is interconnected, each part constantly affecting every other part;
- Therefore, it's not possible to do just one thing, anywhere, at any time.
- Everything we have been able to observe is interconnected with everything else as part of one system, which we call the universe;
- Therefore, by definition, everything in the universe is working together in fulfillment of a purpose.
- Everything that we can observe in this universe, rather than wearing down like a machine as we were told to expect, appears to be increasing in complexity;
- The most complex systems are living systems;
- Therefore, the apparent purpose of the universe is the development and maintenance of living systems.
- Each living system is the harmonious interaction of thousands of elements, working together to sustain the system and

interact with others in increasing complexity.[17]

These ideas have emerged over time, based on the observations of hundreds of people looking at thousands of different aspects of Nature—both on planet Earth and in space.

The implications of this understanding are staggering. They mean that the underlying model of empire culture is false—that everything we've been trained to believe about humanity and our need to "own" and "control" our resources if we are to survive is unfounded. Instead, life happens as the result of harmonious interactions that can't be controlled!

More than that, multiple experiments and observations have demonstrated that any attempt by human beings to control any aspect of a living system causes more harm than good. In other words, our many efforts to "rule over" Nature—like killing off pests, damming up rivers, taking a medicine, clear-cutting forests—cause ever more problems over the long haul, even if apparently achieving the solutions that were intended in the short term.

Also during the 20th century, another field of science was developing. Called quantum mechanics, this field has focused on the incredibly

---

[17] Physics professor Fritjof Capra lays these points out beautifully in his *The Web of Life.*

tiny sets of interactions that make up the systems we call atoms. And again, hundreds of observers, across thousands of observations and experiments (and again, using their own jargon and mathematics), have come up with some basic understandings of how things work that are in direct contradiction to what we've been trained to believe. Among these new understandings are:

- Matter and energy are constantly changing back and forth;
- Therefore they are basically the same stuff, changing form.
- The form they show up as in a given situation depends on whether they are being observed;
- Observation is a function of awareness, or consciousness;
- Therefore the presence or absence of matter or energy at any one place in the universe depends on the presence or absence of an observer, a conscious being.
- Therefore the universe and world that we experience must be either
  o A self-aware conscious entity whose form is matter and energy,[18] *or*
  o The product of a conscious entity,[19] *or*

---

[18] See, for example, *The Self-Aware Universe*, by quantum mechanics professor Amit Goswami.

o Pure consciousness itself, becoming
increasingly complex and forming living systems, including humanity,
through which it is becoming self-
aware.[20]

This new understanding of how the universe works and what it may actually be points,
again, to a very different role for humanity in
the world than we've been trained to think. Far
from justifying our culturally-defined role as
"lord of all we survey"[21] it raises powerful questions, like:

- If consciousness is present everywhere,
  throughout the universe—as it must be for
  there to be matter or energy anywhere in
  the universe—then how can we call an an-
  imal or plant, or even a cell "unconscious"
  or "nonsentient"?
- If conscious observation shapes matter
  and energy, then where does the human
  mind fit into that? Are we shaping the

---

[19] See the work of theoretical physicist Rev. John
Polkinghorne, especially *Quantum Physics and Theology.*

[20] See anything by quantum physicist Fred Alan Wolf
or *The Quantum Self* by Danah Zohar.

[21] It doesn't necessarily contradict the biblical
statement that humanity "has dominion" over other
things because, if the observer is the deciding factor and
humanity is the observer than we are the deciding factor.

matter and energy around us with our observations and thoughts?

- If electrons and photons respond to the presence of people in the laboratory, what do they do in the rest of the world?[22]

So, paradoxically again, the technology developed within empire culture has provided us with tools that demonstrate that the assumptions underlying the culture's claims of need for "control" and "hegemony" in a chaotic, unsupportive universe are unfounded.

The sciences of the 20th century have proven what the wise elders of the Anatolian cultures understood intuitively: that, across the universe, many complex but harmonious relationships work together for the wellbeing of any living being—whether it be a forest, an ocean, or a human body.

The people of the Neolithic era, and in many "primitive" cultures today, understood intuitively what we are discovering in our modern sciences: that nobody runs the show; no one has to be in control or own things or run things to fit a certain standard for everything to work out harmoniously.

---

[22] This question is explored in the Global Consciousness Project: Princeton engineers linking computers using random number generators to measure how much the collective mind of humanity can change the pattern.

They understood what we are only beginning to realize today, in our laboratories and in our businesses: that not only is nobody in charge,[23] nobody has to be, because the successful maintenance of any system is a result of the harmonious relationships within and around it.

---

[23] As a minister I'm well aware that this material may sound like I'm saying God does not participate in the universe. Not at all. I (along with others like me) am saying God does not "rule" the universe the way a king, dictator, or emperor might rule his people. Our current science tells us that no being is sitting on a throne dictating what happens to every individual. Instead we are learning something even more wonderful, more awesome: the universe is the unfolding expression of a form of intelligence, wisdom, and support that is so grand and great we can't even begin to comprehend it! And it is also unfolding as each and every one of us, every moment, as we discover who and what we really are and are capable of being. See my books *One Law* and *As We Think So We Are,* published by Beyond Words, or *The Power of Creative Thought* (Portal Center Press) for more about how this works.

Considering a New Way

Today, the world is being inundated with a flood of images, words, and music, generated in the U.S. and promulgated through the myriad information technologies that define the current Communications Age. People all over the world, in virtually every cafe and hotel, and in many homes, watch programs on television that describe what can only be called an artificial culture.

Children in the U.S. and all over the world spend hours every day observing this culture. They see "contests" that have been staged, "reality" shows in which actors live out scripts in improbable situations, "comedies" in which people deal with major life issues as if they were jokes, and "dramas" and "news" programs that focus almost entirely on death and destruction. They see people living in homes and driving cars far beyond the means of most Americans, with explicit sexuality and violence in virtually all entertainment, and most are convinced that this is the way Americans live—or wish they did.

This artificial culture is definitely *not* the American Way. Yet, to the majority of the world, including most Americans themselves, it seems as if it must be. After all, if the stories people tell are the way they transmit their culture, then our stories must be a description of the way we believe life ought to be lived.

Recently, however, some of us have broken out of our media-induced hypnotic trance. Waking up and looking at the mess around us—the destroyed families, farmlands, rivers, and forests, the debt load carried by individuals and our government, the violence in our schools and cities, the destructiveness of the weapons our military brandishes—we wonder what has happened to our country. The assumption of an ever-brighter future has begun to ring hollow as we see more and more Americans living in poverty, with little hope of escape. And, we ask, what could happen to us— and to the world—if we continue on this path?

Our concern makes the lessons of the past seem worth exploring, rather than ignoring. Some of us are wondering if there isn't something worth learning from those ancestors we've called "backwards" and "primitive" for so long.

Tradition, the thing that the children of our immigrant forebears sought so hard to avoid, doesn't seem like such a dirty word any more.

Maybe being "modern" doesn't mean we have all the answers, after all.[24]

Historically, most Americans are, or have descended from, the Caucasians described in the previous section.[25] We, too, take "what we want when we want it." Many American men discount and even beat the women who care for them. Our "cowboy culture" is very like that of the Caucasian-Semites—and for many of the same reasons. America's street gangs are direct mirrors of those lost boys trying desperately to survive into manhood—and have been since the early nineteenth century.[26] So, too, our militant patriots. For too many of us, the bully on the street or in the school-yard taught us that to be weak was dangerous, and looking strong and controlling everything around us is necessary for survival. Like the lost boys of the Caucasus, we've grown up without much needed security and guidance.

But the lessons of history teach us that the pattern of invasion and empire is a pattern of

---

[24] Paul Ray describes this group as "Cultural Creatives" in his book by that name (co-authored with Sherry Anderson, 2000), suggesting that as many as 80 million Americans were thinking this way in 2008.

[25] Today there are more people of other races here.

[26] As so brilliantly, and violently, demonstrated in Dickens' *Oliver Twist,* Bernstein's *West Side Story,* and the films *Blackboard Jungle* and *The Gangs of New York.*

ongoing destruction—insecure and not at all stable. And the new sciences have confirmed it.

The founders of America understood the need to avoid a despotic ruler, which is why they created a federation of independent, mutually supportive, relatively independent states—a model that has been imitated by other countries and the European Union, since. But, in our fear, we've forgotten what the founders knew and are steadily reverting to the old model of authoritarian leadership.

Will we change it? Can we? Or, in spite of all the evidence telling us it doesn't work, are we all too trapped in the Caucasian "conquer or die" model?

If so, it's not because we know what it means to be invaded. Part of America's greatness derives from the fact that, since 1812, we have not been invaded. There's been no foreign invader on American soil for over 200 years.[27] Very few places in the world can say that—and very few places have enjoyed the economic

---

[27] The border battles with Mexico in the 1890s were mere skirmishes. Pearl Harbor, though it housed part of the US Navy, is on an island that most Americans hadn't even heard of in 1940, 3000 miles away from the continent, and so doesn't count as an invasion of American soil. And the Twin Towers remain a mystery: Saudis flew the planes; Iraq was blamed; US workers "reconditioned" the buildings a few weeks before, and many think there's traces of a demolition chemical (thermite?) in the ruins.

prosperity and technological development that have been possible as a result.

Unfortunately, part of the reason we've been able to have such an extended period of undisturbed peace at home is because we've fought our wars elsewhere. And, having won the first few and now lost a couple, our generals and youthful engineers have built a huge military on the same philosophy of "expand and control" that Caucasians have relied on across history.

Our government's fear of the possibility that we might have enemies out to destroy our nation, has caused it to divert huge amounts of resources, so we have armed ourselves to the point of destroying all life on the planet. We've armed our allies, as well, giving them lots of "foreign aid," and building US military bases in dozens of countries, so they will remain allied with our interests and not switch sides.

Seeking an Answer

In the face of all this, and with the belief that we really do have enemies, can we really, seriously, think about changing our way of being? Is deciding to change our relationships with other countries the answer? Is that the route to world peace? To the survival of humanity on this planet?

If we look at the present world situation in the context of the above history, we can see that our current mode of operation is doomed to failure. Most of American culture—along with those cultures that are influenced by our Communications Era technologies—is operating from assumptions about the world that emphasize fear and control, which, the historical record shows us, leads to collapse and destruction.

Yet, when we look at how we have progressed in this country, we see that the characteristics of trust, stewardship, and cooperative effort have been essential ingredients to our creative ingenuity. America's successes—in our start-up companies, our research teams, our gigantic building projects, our space program—all have been the result of operating from those three qualities.

And, if we look at the cultures that have sustained their people for thousands of years, maintaining secure populations with plenty of time for art and music and loving one another (in a few remaining places, like parts of Bali, Polynesia, traditional indigenous people of the Arctic and Australia, and much of modern Scandinavia), we see the same characteristics: communities of people working together based on trust, stewardship of resources, and cooperation.

From Command-Control to Community

So, what does this mean for the future?

It looks like, if we want to shift from our current, mutually destructive mode of operating in the world, we need to act like a start-up company or a sustainable culture. We need to reestablish trust, stewardship, and cooperation as our norm.

In this Information Age, we can see that the essential mechanism for cooperation—a means of communication—is in place around the world. We have television and radio, the Internet, satellites, wireless systems, and direct-dial telephones. What's missing is the basis for trust and a pattern of stewardship.

Because of the nature of empire culture, few of us have had the opportunity to experience the satisfaction that a cooperative, rather than competitive, work and learning environment can bring. We've been schooled and employed in "command-&-control" environments, trained to achieve specific objectives, usually selected by someone else, to keep the institution going. No trust allowed in these places.

This experience is why, when people like Peter Senge,[28] or Scott Peck,[29] or their stu-

---

[28] Founder of MIT's Center for Learning Organizations and author of *The Fifth Discipline* and *Presence.*

[29] Community Development pioneer and author of *A Different Drum.*

dents, like Joe Jaworsky[30] and Kaz Gozdz,[31] tell us that it's possible to create a work environment where the process of individual development and emotional security is the most important factor in the institution's success, most folks have a hard time believing them.

But it's true. When a group of people are given the opportunity to break through the surface to what really matters, and then are given the space to learn and create and produce from that deeper understanding, organizational miracles do happen.

The process of forming that kind of community is straightforward, though not always easy. Scott Peck practiced it hundreds of times in the 1980s and '90s, as described in his book, *A Different Drum*. His stages, from the casual interactions of what he calls pseudo-community, through the breaking up into a chaotic cacophony of ideas and points of view, into the empty silence of "what do we do now?", leads consistently to the formation of what he calls "authentic community." With the right facilitation, it happens every time: for teams in the workplace, volunteers in nonprofits, leaders

---

[30] Founder of the American Leadership Forum and author of *Synchronicity*.

[31] Coiner of the term "Deliberately Developmental Learning Organizations (DDLO) and author of *Community Building: Renewing Spirit in Business*.

in the military, and attendees at a weekend workshop.

The second piece – and this is where the work of Senge and Gozdz come in – is to create a process for the group to be discovering, creating, and learning – individually and collectively – and so become more productive and effective in achieving their personal and organizational intentions.[32]

When both of these are in place, then the potential for accomplishment is overwhelmingly enhanced. What's more, individuals begin to discover inner resources they didn't know they had. They begin to become what Senge, Gozdz, and Jaworsky call, "Sourcing Leaders." Free of the need to keep up pretentions and barriers, they access an inner wisdom that guides them through uncharted territory—much as the wisdom of the Anatolian elders guided their people.

When that happens, the organization as a whole begins to function at a level previously thought impossible—as Steve Macadam, the recently-retired CEO of the multinational corporation Enpro, discovered and now teaches,

---

[32] The effectiveness of this approach is detailed in the book *An Everyone Culture* by Robert Kegan and Lisa Lahey.

along with a score of other similarly enlightened executives.[33]

From Conflict to Cooperation

You see, the only real conflict is within our own minds. It's between what we've been taught must be the case and what history shows (and our inner self knows) really is the case. As the Silicon Valley startups of the 1980s – 2000s demonstrated over and over again, when the artificial barriers imposed by empire culture's systems of command-and-control are released, huge potentials in learning and creativity are realized.

Because of those barriers, we feel like we're almost in a "Catch-22." We don't believe we can trust each other because we believe everyone else in the world wants to expand over and control everyone else. But history has shown us that we have to trust one another in order to break that very pattern of invasion and empire.

An example of breaking through this conundrum may be seen in the relationship between Kennedy and Kruschev during the Cuban Missile Crisis. At first, they had none of the necessary ingredients: no way to communicate except through spies and ambassadors, no shared resources to steward, nor any basis for

[33] The Inner MBA program, sponsored by Sounds True publishing and New York University.

trust, and hence no way to cooperate. Each of them had advisors telling them that the other wanted nothing more than to destroy them completely, now. But each of them knew that once started, this war would leave no winner. It was that realization, the common desire to preserve the resources of life and land in their countries, which gave them a basis for moving forward. It was this common desire that motivated them to use the only communications tools available, a direct telephone line. This, ultimately, allowed them to come to a cooperative agreement regarding the missiles in Cuba—and established a permanent direct communications link between the two world leaders.[34]

A Longer View

Often, the answer to a question about the present doesn't lie in the present, but in some combination of the past, the present, and a future possibility. Einstein (along with a couple of other geniuses) is frequently quoted as saying "you can't solve a problem at the level of the problem." We have to step outside of a problem and look at it from a different angle to be able to see the connections and the possibilities that are already within it.

---

[34] Kevin Costner's film, *13 Days,* poignantly illustrates this process.

Taking that longer view—of past, present, and possible future—brings us to a whole new set of questions. If the assumptions we've been trained to build our lives around are inaccurate; if there really is no need to be "in control" to be safe; then the door is open to explore a wide range of alternatives.

We've seen that the qualities of trust, stewardship, and cooperation have been essential ingredients of long-term sustainable cultures, as well as our past successes. Is there a way we can apply them, today?

We've learned from studying communities, businesses, and other human systems that the way to bring people together in a cooperative effort is to focus everyone's attention on something bigger than they are that will benefit all of them. That's how the space program happened in the U.S. and the Marshall Plan was implemented between the U.S., Japan, and Europe. It's also how the pre-Caucasian cultures built their huge temples, irrigation systems, and sewer-systems. Can we use that knowledge?

What would happen if, instead of trying to control others out of fear, we learned to embrace our fears and work with those others whom we feared? Would it make it possible to turn this pattern of the past around?

Looking Forward to a Possibility

Is there anything we have in common that could be a shared focus for humanity as a whole? In this world of dissonance and violence is there anything we can agree upon? Anything that would undo the military and ecological impasse we're at?

Well, actually, there is. Apart from global climate change—which we may or may not be able to affect—and the inundation of plastic wastes, the technology to address which is only now emerging[35], we're all affected by our dependence on oil for transportation, raw materials, and electricity. And access to oil is a big part of the problem in Asia and the Middle East—affecting both sides of the issues there.

Oil as a Starting Point

As usual, the statement of the problem suggests a solution. What would happen if a large number of nations began a cooperative ef-

---

[35] A wonderful YouTube video summarizing the current status of plastic recycling may be found at: https://youtu.be/D7vRm1E5rn0

fort to wean themselves off oil as fuel—using it solely as stock for plastics and related materials—within five years? Does that sound as impossible as putting a man on the moon by 1969 did in 1961?

What would happen if, as part of that effort, opportunities were provided for boys and men in the Middle East who are being trained in the Empire Way to meet and work with Muslims from other parts of the world where the Invasion & Empire model is no longer the norm?

What would happen if, instead of trying to make Iraq and Afghanistan part of the American hegemony, we came up with a mutual "Marshall Plan" that took all countries off the oil standard?

One thing that would happen is that the US government's concern about oil being tied to the euro (European Economic Union money)[36] rather than the US dollar would be immediately diminished, because oil would no longer be so essential to our national wellbeing. Another thing that might happen is that the oil-producing countries, instead of absorbing most of the wealth of most of the rest of the world,

---

[36] Iraq's Saddam Hussein made the shift from accepting dollars to accepting euros in 2000, which many analysts consider the real reason for our government's war against him, since it would contribute dramatically to the devaluing of the dollar.

might begin to share that wealth as a strategy for mutual survival. The one thing we can count on happening with such an effort is a major upswing in the economies of all the nations involved, as new companies are formed and new possibilities emerge out of the new technologies and processes that are implemented.

Then, once we've established a basis for trust, using the existing means of communication, we can explore other ways to work cooperatively while stewarding our resources—like, say, cleaning up the world's lakes and rivers? Or reversing desertification? They're huge projects, but the technologies for all of them exist, today.

All it takes is the willingness to trust, steward our resources, and cooperate in creating something that didn't exist before—which are the primary lessons of the Anatolian Way, and the essence and greatness of the American Way.

Design through Participation

What would it take for a large number of nations working together to get themselves off of petroleum as their primary fuel source?

The design process is always the same, whether for a meal, an invasion, or a multinational project. The first step is to get clear about your intentions. Then, look at what's needed to accomplish them. An assessment of existing resources follows, with a plan for acquiring the missing pieces. Then it's time to get agreement among all the participants—with a shared commitment to do whatever it takes, within agreed-upon limits, to get the job done. With these in place, it's possible to consider a variety of approaches and select the most promising one. A test of the approach makes sure it will work.

At that point the actual work begins. Periodic "check-ins" are planned and carried out, to determine progress and make necessary modifications along the way. As the project nears completion, a review of all that has been done ensures that nothing important has been left out. And finally, the job is done: Neil Armstrong declares "a giant leap for mankind;" the butler announces "dinner is served;" Steve Jobs demonstrates a smart phone.

Clarifying our Intentions

Why would we want to do this project? What is the benefit to all concerned? These are the questions to ask at this stage.

As the preceding section indicates, the primary benefits of a multinational effort to get off of oil are twofold:

- It would provide an opportunity to build a pattern of trust, communication, cooperation, and stewardship of resources among the nations of the world;
- It would defuse much of the tension in the Middle East by reducing the rest of the world's dependence on that area and creating a different model for the boys and young men of that region.

For the nations involved in the project, it would also be an opportunity to reduce the cash flow out of the country, to develop new, local businesses and industries, and to unite the people in a cooperative effort "bigger than they are" that is not war.

For the nations of the Middle East, the continued use of petroleum for the many wonderful products made from it would ensure a continued stream of income, for a much longer time, while the incredible pressure on them of being the fuel source for the world (and hence a strategic target for the world) would be greatly decreased.

To the extent that the nations involved were able to create media support for the values of trust, stewardship, and cooperation, (rather than violence and conflict) as the norm, a new generation would be raised with a new kind of dream—just as those who were raised on the dream of reaching the moon went on to create the Internet, with its world wide web.

Ultimately, then, such a project would be a giant step toward world peace.

The project would have other benefits as well. To the extent that the new fuels were based on non-burning sustainable resources (e.g. solar electricity, wind, fuel cells, and hydropower), the air would be cleaner and global warming would be slowed. To the extent that funds were shifted from the expansion of weapons systems and the military into this new project, the build-up toward mass destruction would be slowed.

So our statement of intention might read:

> *To shift the world's primary fuel from oil to other, renewable sources and so reduce international violence, global warming, and air pollution, while enhancing the local economies of all participating nations.*

Necessary Resources

What would it take to accomplish this intention? What kind of tools, people, processes, and support systems would be needed to get a significant number of nations off of oil as their primary fuel?

We'd need lots of engineers, of all types, who have experience with the "cooperation-trust-stewardship" model used in hi-tech start-up companies.

We'd need alternatives to oil as fuel—which, over the last 30 years, many individuals and companies have been developing, and which are now, in most cases, functional.

We'd need factories to produce these alter-natives—which, because of the layoffs resulting from the crumpling economies around the world, are empty and available.

We'd need warehouses to store parts and finished products—which, again, are available, but not as necessary as they once were be-cause of the Internet's capability for supporting "just-in-time" systems.

We'd need suppliers of raw materials and parts—which we have if we act soon, before they go out of business because their custom-ers have been disappearing.

We'd need investors, willing to put their dol-lars into socially and environmentally respon-sible projects—which we have in the many "SRF"s around the world, and we could also di-vert some research funds from the military or petroleum-based projects.

We'd need media support for the project: news anchors, talk-show hosts, celebrities, and advertising exec's who understood and appreciated the concept—some of which are already in place, but more of whom would have to be educated in the concept.

We'd need project coordinators within each country (state and national agencies—or bioregional agencies) and among the nations involved (a U.N. agency? Continental agencies?)

But most importantly, we'd need a *willingness* on the part of the people and their governments in every participating nation to do what is needed to make this shift in a mutually supporting cooperative, rather than controlling, competitive, manner.

Acquiring the Missing Pieces

We have all the pieces to accomplish this project in place, right now. All, that is, except the primary one: a willingness on the part of the nations to take it on.

What will it take to convince the governments that their people don't really care if their cars and boats and lawnmowers are powered by gasoline or some other fuel? What will it take for our governments to understand that we'd really prefer clean air and freedom from the fear of mass destruction over having a bigger car—that we only take the car because that's all we get? Plenty of books have been written and polls have been taken that prove it, but somehow the message isn't getting through.

There are always at least three options in every situation like this. In this case, they seem to be:

- form a non-governmental organization and simply begin the work, demonstrating to the governments that it can be effective;
- create a major media campaign to educate the people and their governments about the benefits of the project;
- storm the governments with petitions and demonstrations; or,
- convince a few legislators in a few countries to submit bills to their legislative bodies and begin the process.

As usual, the most effective plan would probably be some combination of the above.

Coming to an Agreement

Given that the only requirement missing for accomplishing this proposed project is the active agreement of the participants, that's clearly where the initial work needs to be done. And it needs to be done soon, because the engineers and facilities won't be available forever.

Such an agreement would include several parts:

- the shared statement of intent for the project;
- which aspects of the project would be undertaken by which nations;
- accepted limits on the resources, effort, and infringements on other nations' sovereignty;
- the pace at which oil purchases from the Middle East will be reduced;
- a target completion date.

Drafting this agreement would have to be the work of skilled negotiators at the international level—perhaps a former officer of the United Nations. The process would take several rounds of both formal and informal meetings, and (based on past history) the final agreement may have to be modified part way through. But it must be done, for it's the heart of the project: there's no way to get to trust-stewardship-cooperation without an underlying agreement.

Making it Work

Each nation would put together its own plan for accomplishing the tasks it's agreed to. Each region within the nation would have its own part to play in that plan.

Where possible, larger nations with excess capability would share resources with smaller, less endowed nations. For example, India now has a huge group of engineers, perhaps the greatest supply of engineers in the world, and may be willing and able to share those with other nations; the U.S. has many patented technologies that may be implemented in other parts of the world. And so forth.

In the U.S., we have several levels of government, each with its own role to play in implementing such a strategy.

- at the federal level, we have patents, funds, licensing, and coordination of regulations;
- at the federal region level, we have regulations;
- at the state level, we have site control, as well as air, soil, and water quality control, transportation management, and regulations and taxation;
- at the district level (inter-county transportation management, soil conservation, water conservation, power, education, etc.), we have a number of overlapping issues that may need to be addressed;
- at the county level, we have land-use, transportation management, regulations and taxation;
- at the city level, we have land-use, transportation management, licensing, and taxation.

A major challenge will be to coordinate action at these various levels of government, with their overlapping concerns and issues, in a timely fashion. It's a big project, but that's the whole idea—taking on something bigger than we can imagine ways to accomplish!

We'll have to be clear and careful not to create more demand for what we're trying stop using—which is to say, we'll have to really look at the alternatives we're putting in place to make sure they don't use more oil to create than they replace. For example, giant wind turbines or large-scale solar systems may, in fact, take more energy to produce than they produce themselves. Nuclear power plants definitely do.

Another major challenge will be to find ways to make this shift in the way we operate non-threatening to those whose lives will be affected—which includes virtually everybody in the U.S., and a significant majority of other nations, as well. Not only do many people drive cars fueled by petroleum derivatives, their goods are transported by diesel-powered trucks and trains. Not only are fuel taxes a significant source of income for the states and cities, the highways on which we drive are maintained with those dollars.[37] And, especially over the

---

[37] The U.S. interstate freeway system, built with Defense Department dollars under the National Defense Transportation Act, has become the arterial system for

recent decades, many homes and buildings are now heated by "clean-burning" petroleum or, in some cases, gasified petroleum.

If an incentive can be provided for turning in or converting used cars, then much of that problem may be addressed fairly easily (that is, it becomes an engineering problem rather than a social one). Trucks are another matter: the little boy in all of us loves those huge, powerful beasts, with their deep, rumbling engines and commanding presence on the roadway. The silent operation of a battery or fuel cell may not be nearly as exciting—or acceptable. And the corporate costs of transition will be phenomenal—subsidies and incentives may be only the beginning, there. As for buildings that are heated by oil—again subsidies and incentives that make the transfer to a less polluting form an obvious money-saver have been proven to do the trick.

If these kinds of solutions become necessary, however, the bulk of funds for the U.S. and other industrialized countries to shift away from oil will be spent, not on designing and manufacturing new technologies, but on convincing people to make the shift.

At this point in the erosion of the democratic republic, for a government to see the value in

the US economy, while our privately owned and operated

such a plan, the stakeholders have to be recognized and appeased. Then leaders can act.

Given that situation, perhaps a different kind of strategy will be needed—akin to Churchill and Roosevelt asking everyone to put their car in the garage and gather all the metal and rubber they could find for the "boys over there" during World War II. An all-out campaign of patriotism mixed with altruism could be the winning strategy for this project; it would be in complete accord with the spirit of our intention—and is very doable, today.

Envisioning Completion

Imagine what it would be like to live in a world where smog is unusual, while cars and trucks are available as needed, easy to drive, and quiet. Imagine that political tension in the Middle East is a non-issue, and all nations are working together in cooperation to optimize our diminishing resources rather than fighting each other for them. Imagine that we've found whole new ways to power our homes and farms and factories—ways which enhance the wellbeing of all.

Imagine these things because they're not only possible, they're feasible.

---

rail systems are deteriorating and even disappearing.

Not only that, doing something like this may be the only way out of the mess we're in today. Cooperation across ancient boundaries, toward a mutually beneficial outcome, learning about each other – and to trust each other – in the process, is the only antidote to the fear that has gone viral in recent years.

So imagine it, please—with all the gratitude, joy, and appreciation for such a world that you can muster.

Imagine it because, as has been demonstrated from time immemorial, we can only achieve that which we can imagine. And, as metaphysicians of all the ages, and now neuroscientists as well, have come to understand, what we imagine with feeling *must* come to pass.

Afterword

The View from 2020

The time to put this book together came during the global CoVid19 "lockdown." For me, as a single working adult, being told not to drive to meetings and lectures opened up lots of time to complete projects such as this. For others, though, these weeks have been filled with fear and pressure: children wanting to see their friends and complaining; active adults feeling much the same way; "sandwich generation" families being cut off from elders who rely on them. No income for weeks at a time. It's been hard.

Then came the eruption immediately following that pressure-cooker time: days and nights filled with protests in the streets. The stimulus was an incident of the horrific brutality against dark-skinned men practiced by the police forces of American cities, which, though once hidden, is now, with handheld cameras and instant communication, all too terribly visible.[38]

That incident may have been the stimulus, but actually, the protestors are reacting to something much deeper than police behavior.

These worldwide protests are really against the control by fear that is the hallmark of the empire culture which is now affecting all of us. George Floyd is EveryMan, under the knee of the empire, saying (all too poignantly, after we've all spent weeks in fear of death by an Acute Respiratory Syndrome), "I Can't Breathe!" until he died.

We can't breathe! He spoke for all of us. The culture we are subject to is no longer a place where the opportunities for riches are reward enough to sacrifice the freedom to live on our own terms, doing meaningful work in loving relationships, safe and secure in homes we have bought or built, in communities that support one another's wellbeing. It's not enough; we can't breathe, and we are dying.

Which is why now, at this time in human history, the ideas presented in this book must be shared.

Now, more than ever, what's needed is a New Way, a way to bring people together to ad-

---

[38] One YouTube video is a graph showing nearly 20,000 killings by U.S. police in the past decade alone: https://youtu.be/8s8O8-_AGKw.

dress a common concern, beyond the divisiveness imposed upon us by a controlling few. A way to function as human beings, rather than simply consumers and wage-slaves.

What's needed is opportunities to experience authentic community where learning and growing lead to breakthroughs in understanding and productivity – and breakdowns of the artificial separations that have been built between us.

What's needed is the kind of global project that is outlined in this book, involving as many people as possible in as many ways as possible, facilitated by people who have one goal in mind: humanity thriving as an integral part of the living system that is this wonderful planet, Earth.

Only then will we know that we can live without the assumptions of fear and control. Only then will we have found the way to build on the best of the past to, once more, base our lives on trust, cooperative effort, stewardship, and the inner wisdom that is available to us all.

Thank you for reading this book, for considering this alternative model of our current situation, and for exploring this project idea with me.

Ruth L Miller, June 2020

About the Author

Ruth L. Miller, Ph.D. integrates new under-standings of culture and consciousness. With degrees in anthropology, environmental studies, cybernetics, and the systems sciences she taught in several colleges and universities. Now, having completed a second career as an ordained New Thought minister, she consults, writes, and speaks on the nature of consciousness and spirituality, and the future of humanity.

Portal
Center
Press

Other Portal Center Press books by Ruth L Miller

Empowered Care, mind-body medicine methods
with Robert B. Newman

Home: choosing humanity's future

Language of Life: solutions to modern crises in an
ancient way of speaking, *with Milt Markewitz & Batya
Podos*

Making the World Go Away: coping in end times

Mary's Power: embracing the divine feminine as the
age of invasion and empire ends

The Power of Creative Thought: Thomas Troward's
metaphysics in the modern world

The Science of Mental Healing: lives and teachings
of America's New Thought healers

Uncommon Prayer

Unlocking the Power of THE SECRET: 10 keys to
transform your thoughts and life

…and check out our many other writers – plus
fiction and spiritual explorations under our
imprint: SPIRITBOOKS

www.portalcenterpress.com